DON'T BACK DOWN

*A Mother's Story Waging War on Her
Son's Diagnosis of Cancer*

BY KATHERINE C. MARTINEZ

Trilogy Christian Publishers

A Wholly Owned Subsidiary of Trinity Broadcasting Network

2442 Michelle Drive

Tustin, CA 92780

For information, address Trilogy Christian Publishing

Rights Department, 2442 Michelle Drive, Tustin, CA 92780.

Trilogy Christian Publishing/ TBN and colophon are trademarks of Trinity Broadcasting Network.

For information about special discounts for bulk purchases, please contact Trilogy Christian Publishing.

10 9 8 7 6 5 4 3 2 1

Library of Congress Cataloging-in-Publication Data is available.

ISBN 979-8-89041-569-1

ISBN 79-8-89041-570-7 (ebook)

Dedication

I dedicate this book to the Lord, who encouraged me to write it.

And to my youngest son. God knows you've endured more than most, but He remains faithful through it all.

Dad and Mom—thank you for believing in me.

To my family and friends who helped me get this book off the ground.

This book is also for anyone who feels like there is no hope. There is.

Table of Contents

Preface

In no way, shape, or form is this book intended to undermine or make light of any physical illness someone may be experiencing right now or even in the past. This is my account of how I dealt with things when my son was not in good health.

This book is not a guide or details of a formula on how to deal with attacks from the enemy on your physical body or anyone else's. This book intends to let you know that you don't have to put up with the devil's wiles—both now and in the future.

I tried to write this book in chronological order as I remembered how events unfolded. In some of these chapters, you will find that some events may have occurred simultaneously or months ahead, but they all tie into one another.

Throughout this book, medical terminology is not used. Primarily, it is because I'm not a medical professional, and I want the reader to understand that although my son faced what he did, this story can be applied to any situation you or a loved one may be facing.

Don't Back Down

The voice of the Lord is powerful; the
voice of the Lord is full of majesty.

Psalm 27:4

With men this is impossible, but with God
all things are possible.

Matthew 19:26

Heaven and earth shall pass away, but my
words shall not pass away.

Matthew 24:35

Introduction

From the very beginning of writing this book, it is as if it was just yesterday that we faced the enemy head-on. Each time I recall every detail the Holy Spirit brought to my remembrance of God's goodness during that trial, I can't help but cry. It's almost like in the Spirit I was watching a real-life story unfold. Maybe this doesn't make sense because it was real. I was trying to process it all while fighting in the Spirit. However, I already knew the ending from the start. It took some time for my mind to catch up with what I felt inside, but when I caught on and imagined His Word coming alive inside of me, everything began to line up accordingly.

In the book of Haggai, God tells us He will rebuke the Devourer for our sake. I am reminded of the story in the Word of God about a widow and her only child. Uncertain of the future for her and her child, the woman obeyed the Lord amid their dire need. I thank the Lord for providing an example to follow in a time of crisis.

1 Kings 17 tells the story of a widow who did not see a way out of her current situation. She did what came naturally and did all she could to keep her and her only son alive. Driven by the perception that their last days on Earth

would quickly arrive, the widow picked up sticks to help prepare what could be one last meal. Then, the prophet Elijah arrived and instructed the widow to bring him water and bread before she made a meal for herself and her son. In obedience to the Word of the Lord, the widow set out to prepare his meal.

What a glorious day this was for the widow; although, she didn't know it at the time. She heard God when He said He was sending the prophet, but for a moment, she couldn't see getting past death (verse 12). But she chose to believe God amid it all, and as she was on her way, the prophet Elijah brought her great news that God promised to keep the meal coming and the cruse of oil full (verse 14).

As time went on, the widow's son became very ill and died. Distraught and confused, the widow imagined this occasion happened due to some past sin. Because of the relationship Elijah had with God, Elijah took the boy to an upstairs room and cried out to God to bring the boy back to life. The Lord heard Elijah's cry, and the boy became alive and well again. The widow's response to Elijah gives us a glimpse into the power of God's Word when she says in verse 24, "Now I know that you are a man of God and that the word of the Lord from your mouth is the truth."

Introduction

Much like the widow, I, too, had to rely heavily on God's Word despite apparent circumstances staring at us right in the face. I had to rely on people to help me, which was something I wasn't used to. Sometimes, I felt alone and uncertain about how to provide the care my son needed—not equipped to help my son. God sent many wonderful people who walked alongside and provided guidance. I had to believe and trust God no matter what. Above all, I had to receive God's healing for both of us, even though I couldn't see it in the natural. For you see, II Corinthians 5:7 says, "For we walk by faith, not by sight."

God does speak to us directly, but He uses people to get his messages across to us. Through the leading of the Holy Spirit, seeking out people and ministries with like-minded faith, and engulfing myself in the written word of God, I overcame mental and spiritual obstacles that sometimes would not allow me to see God's goodness on the other side. It took staying constantly connected to God, both before and after, to know and see the full manifestation of God's unfailing love. And because I chose to stay steadfast and connected to everything God has laid out for me, God's Word was able to take root in my spirit so that I could see the unseen.

Chapter 1

THE BEGINNING

And the LORD went before them by day in a pillar of a cloud, to lead them the way; and by night in a pillar of fire, to give them light; to go by day and night: He took not away the pillar of the cloud by day, nor the pillar of fire by night, from before the people.

Exodus 13:21-22

It was Tuesday just before noon; I got a call from school that my son had fainted and hit the back of his head so hard on the ground that he got quite a bump. Previously, he had been experiencing other unusual symptoms that were not normal for him. He had seen a doctor a few weeks before to see what could be causing him to feel not like himself, but nothing was conclusive.

When I arrived at school, he was very upset and could barely walk. The staff explained to me briefly what happened—how and where he fell. Because the bump on the back of his head was so large, we needed to see if that caused any sort of trauma. I needed to take him to the emergency room to have him checked out.

Before we headed to the hospital, his dear high school principal at that time prayed for my son that all would be well. I truly believe in my heart that his prayer set the stage for the victory that was down the road. Although it was not clear at the time what my son would face, it was reassuring to be surrounded by faith; his prayer was a defining moment in many ways because it set in motion the placement of all the events that would lead to my son's miraculous recovery, which brought about God's complete healing manifestation.

After the principal prayed, we were off to the emergency room. When we arrived, my son could hardly stand up. I managed to get him in a wheelchair and went through the check-in process. He was placed in a holding room in the meantime while being scheduled for a scan of his head focused on the area where he had that large bump.

While waiting in the room before the scan, my son looked calm. I didn't know what to make of anything and wondered what could be wrong. Finally, the time came for him to get the scan. They allowed me to be in there with him which was fine.

Suddenly, one of the nurses who were in the room began to ask me questions about how he had been feeling and if he had been experiencing any unusual symptoms. I mentioned that he had. She jotted down a few notes and walked out of the room. The scan was completed, and we went back to the holding area.

There were a few windows where I could look out at the nurses' station, and I could see the nurse who spoke to me earlier, talking to the head nurse and looking over to our room. When I walked outside to see if they could tell me something about the scan, the head nurse said she had some bad news for me. She told me that my son had a large mass on the back of his brain and that this mass was what probably caused him to faint and why he had been experiencing other unusual symptoms. I went back inside and walked to where my son was lying and told him what the nurse told me. We cried for a bit, but then we both seemed to get our bearings in order.

I can't imagine, even to this day, what may have been going through my son's mind. Just five years prior, he lost his father to a deadly disease. And now this. No, things would be different, and we both knew it. We knew that, whether our minds caught up with our hearts or not, we needed to trust God.

Months if not a year before, I had been drawing close to the Lord because I wanted to know him in a much deeper way. Through prayer, fasting, and daily reading of God's Word, my relationship with the Lord grew increasingly stronger. So, when the news of what my son might have had come, there was no room for tears. I put on God's armor for me and fashioned myself mentally and spiritually as a warrior. And yes, there were scary times when I didn't feel like a warrior nor sounded like one for that matter. But I needed to stay in tune with the leading of the Holy Spirit if we were going to get through this time successfully.

I didn't know how everything would unfold; however, I knew that I could not passively sit by and let this situation dictate my reactions to things. No, it was time to fight and to fight the way God wanted me to. Along the way, some people and ministries helped us not to go this alone, and God was with us every step of the way.

Chapter 2

STEP 1

My sheep hear my voice, and I know them, and they follow me: And I give unto them eternal life, and they shall never perish, neither shall any man pluck them out of my hand.

John 10:27-28

Don't believe everything you hear. This is hard to understand and goes against everything we have been taught, but it's essential if you have any chance of fighting the enemy.

I must admit that my faith and confidence in doctors and medical staff, in general, is slim. Some reasons will not be explained in this book as to why I feel this way; however, because they are just as human as the next person, they too need our prayers. Because medical personnel follows a set of rules, guidelines, and protocols, many times the conventional aspect of the profession may not lend to employing a different resource for healing aside from what they've studied and are familiar with in their years of practice.

Since we are true believers in Christ who receive and live by what was done at the cross for us, we are not subject nor bound to follow the same rules of seeing things. 1 Corinthians 2:13-16 says:

> Which things also we speak, not in words which man's wisdom teacheth, but which the Holy Spirit teacheth; comparing spiritual things with spiritual. But the natural man receiveth not the things of the Spirit of God: for they are foolishness unto him; neither can he know them because they are spiritually discerned. But he that is spiritual judgeth all things, yet he is judged of no man. For who hath known the mind of the Lord, that he may instruct him? But we have the mind of Christ.

The discovery of the mass on my son's brain set in motion a series of events that included relieving some of the pressure from behind his head and scans with surgery to follow more than likely. It's hard to believe that just a few hours before, my son was hanging out with his friends, and then a few hours later, they discovered a brain tumor. It doesn't end there, and the enemy stops at nothing to get you to deny God's wonder-working power. In the middle of everything, it seemed as though the weight of the world suddenly descended upon my shoulders. I had to activate my faith, it was time to grow up and show up, so to speak. Whose report am I to believe? I chose to believe the report of the Lord (Isaiah 53:1) who tells me: "Surely he has borne our griefs and carried our sorrows, yet we did esteem him stricken, smitten of God, and afflicted. But he was wounded for our transgressions, he was bruised for our iniquities; the chastisement of our peace was upon him; and by his stripes, we are healed." Halleluiah! It's settled. It's done. It's been dealt with. I'm not to worry. I'm not to be concerned. My son has a purpose, and nothing is going to stop the plan God has for his life. Amen! The Bible tells us in 1 Peter 5:8: "Be sober, be vigilant, because your adversary the devil, as a roaring lion, walketh about, seeking whom he may devour."

It was time to put my faith into action. I had to align with what God's Word says not what the circumstance was telling me. God, not man, has the final say. Nothing can snatch us from God's hands. Amen!

I'm so glad my son attended a Christian school. Everyone at his school, from the students to the parents, to the faculty, and the staff was exceptional, helpful, kind, and loving. The superintendent and the principal came by to see my son. I can still see their smile and assurance. They prayed for my son and offered their support. And my son's friends were no exception, too. Just before evening, some of his friends and their parents came by to see him and cheer him up. They, along with everyone at the school, played a tremendous role in his life-saving recovery. It was good to see them there and to see their childlike faith at work. I know they felt terrible for him. But that visit cheered him up.

Early in the evening, my son had minor surgery to relieve the pressure from his brain. And while he recovered a bit, later he went through a lengthy scan from head to toe, with a primary focus on his brain and spine. I didn't want to talk to anyone or see anyone while walking down that long corridor and into a room where the MRI machine was. I stayed in that room with him while he went through the scan. For about three or more hours, in that noisy and somewhat dark room, I prayed scriptures over him. Each time he had one of those scans, I would sit in the room, with my Bible in hand, reading scripture after scripture, speaking blessings and life over my son.

> No weapon that is formed against thee shall prosper; and every tongue that shall rise against thee in judgment thou shalt condemn. This is the heritage of the servants of the Lord, and their righteousness is of me, saith the Lord.
>
> **Isaiah 54:17**

Step 1

Later, as the doctors were making their patient visits just outside the patient's room, they came by my son's room and wanted to talk with me. The doctors mentioned that the scans revealed my son had a malignant brain tumor and a spot on his lower spine. They mentioned that typically with this type of tumor, there will be a diseased area in the spine. It wasn't certain that the spot, which was the size of a pen head, was cancerous, but they indicated more than likely that it was. They also mentioned surgery would be scheduled to remove the tumor.

At that moment, upon hearing what my son might have, I maintained that warrior spirit from earlier. Although the doctors were speaking to me, in my spirit I began to wage war on the enemy. There was not going to be anymore more sitting on the sidelines, so to speak, like I did when my husband went through what he did. I was not going to keep silent and let every negative word sink in me until it consumed me with fear. No, something in me rose and taught me how to stand amid a tumultuous storm.

Before this, a series of blood work was performed, and I was not told what it revealed. So, while the grim report was communicated to me, I didn't cry, pass out, or even have a surprised look on my face. Nor did I let out a yell so unspeakable as I did when my husband was diagnosed many years ago. I said the first thing that came to my mind that was important to me and became very important throughout. I asked about the series of blood work taken and what were the results of them. The question was not for mere knowledge purposes or to face the facts. No, my question was directed at the mountain right in front of me and my son. I wasn't pointing a finger at God and asking Him, telling Him, how wrong He was and how He had to fix this. I looked the enemy square in the eye and said that I was not a coward. I will not run or hide in a corner. The fight is on. Not a fight for a cure, because Jesus already paid the price for that. I wasn't playing games. And the enemy was not going to have my son.

After the doctors left, I went back into my son's room. I sat there and just thought for a long while wondering what I was going to do. Out of desperation, because time was of the essence, I walked back outside and began to call around other hospitals my son could go to for help. I wasn't comfortable at all with where he was staying. I didn't know what I was doing necessarily, but I was making plans already, setting things in motion in the right direction. One doctor saw me outside and asked what I was doing. I told him I was trying to look for other places where my son could go to get better care. He told me I was tired and that I should get some sleep and just walked away. If I ever needed any confirmation about anything, that, among other things, was the one.

With no luck getting anywhere or finding the answers I needed, I went back inside my son's room and prayed for him. He had no idea exactly what was going on. In his young teenage mind, he just wanted to be out of the hospital and with his friends. So, God would honor that and meet him where he was. Even though time seemed to slow down, and things took a while to get him to that point, God, as always, came through. He came through in ways I could never imagine.

While settling in for the night, I briefly glanced at my phone. I could see many messages from dear loved ones and some of my son's friends' parents. Because there was just so much to process mentally at that time, sending a reply was not possible. So, I lay down and closed my eyes to try to get some sleep. However, one message caught my attention, and I could hardly sleep just thinking about it. I couldn't wait for morning to arrive.

Chapter 3

SUNSHINE

It is of the LORD's mercies that we are not consumed because his compassions fail not. They are new every morning: great is thy faithfulness.

Lamentations 3:22-23

The day started nice and sunny. My eldest son had spent the night with us there in my son's hospital room. He woke up bright and early and headed out to begin his workday. My son was still asleep, probably tired from the long scan and the minor surgery performed the night before.

While he lay there, I took my phone out and began reading some of my text messages. I came to the message that caught my attention the night before. It was from a sweet parent who was apologetically suggesting that I consider another surgeon. We hadn't met each other yet, but for me, she was like a true friend should be. She mentioned that her husband works at the hospital where a great surgeon currently resides. My reply was that I was open to considering this surgeon since I did not feel comfortable with the one who was scheduled to perform the surgery.

Looking back, it was nothing short of a miracle having this famous surgeon reside in our city. He is well known not only throughout the US but in other parts of the world. God uses people to get his message across. I wasn't listening to the inner voice. He had to get my attention somehow. So, God prepared a way and used willing vessels such as this sweet parent to get my attention. Thank you, Jesus.

As soon as she provided me with the surgeon's number, I called when office hours were available. Call after call and message after message, I was not able to get a hold of anyone. Rightfully so, with such a person as him. Time was drawing close when we were told when the surgeon would be in to talk to us. I wasn't sure what I was going to say and how the doctor would react to me letting her know that my son would not be having surgery there.

A little after 1:00 p.m., there was still no call back from the surgeon's office. I paced the floor a bit and tried to rehearse in my mind the speech I would be giving and if it was just enough not to receive any pushback from the doctor. Time ran out and the surgeon, along with another doctor, walked into the room. Before any in-depth discussions occurred, I boldly confessed that my son would not be having the operation at this hospital. The doctor asked whom I had in mind to perform the surgery. I gave her the name and she looked past me and glanced over to where the other doctor was standing a few feet on the side of me. She asked me why I chose the other surgeon and not to be disrespectful, I told her I needed someone with more confidence to perform the surgery.

To my surprise, she could not disagree. The doctor honored my wishes. And before we could talk about anything else, the other doctor asked if I had been in communication with the other surgeon. I mentioned I had not been able to get a hold of anyone. He told me not to worry about anything. He would be contacting the office for us and before you know it, two hours later my son is in an ambulance and off to the other hospital. I followed close by in my car. There was no looking back and no regrets. In my heart, I know the right thing was done.

Chapter 4

THE BEGINNING OF THE BEGINNING

Then a great multitude followed Him because they saw His signs which He performed on those who were diseased.

John 6:2

When we arrived at the hospital, it was hard to believe we were there. It was a completely different atmosphere both aesthetically and spiritually. Who would have guessed that this would become the place where everything started? My son's healing, my healing perspective, and my faith would be challenged and challenged by others.

When my son was settled in his room, I felt at peace. It came and went throughout this whole time, but peace persisted. The surgeon came by my son's room and introduced himself to us. He was a bubbly man with a great big smile. His demeanor was comforting and seemed sure of himself. As he sat across the room and my son on the hospital bed, he began to expound on his years of experience as a surgeon. Of all the surgeries he performed, he remarked, only one stood out to be not as successful as he would have liked. Still with his fingers on his lips, cupped in a triangle shape, he knew it would be okay to perform the surgery.

Looking back a bit, one of my frustrations in managing, so to speak, my husband's health and how it was received, was that it seemed like many in the medical field were afraid to do anything. I'm not sure where that comes from, but in the end, my husband was at a facility that did all it could, making no promises. That's all I ever wanted. How could I fault someone for something they had nothing to do with nor could not control? I just wanted someone to try and do something.

So, this surgeon's confession was much appreciated. He is not God. He does not have the last say. God created him and blessed him with the ability to do what very few could ever attempt to do or imagine. He saw his talent and passion and went for it!

After he left, I felt good about that decision. In my heart, I knew my son would be in good hands. We just needed to get out of the negativity that was beginning to circle my son. I think about the Bible and how many people were hidden, went into hiding, and had to look for a place to find rest, reassurance, and for the most part, protection. As mentioned in a previous chapter, because the Devil roams around seeking to destroy us, I needed to remain vigilant and sensitive to the voice of the Holy Spirit to guide my next steps.

Being a loving parent, we try our hardest to protect our children from harm. And the way it comes physically or mentally, we keep careful watch over them. And parents' everyday vigilance over their children is not bound to the home. I remember on several occasions when our boys were very young, and our family outings consisted of time near water - how eager they wanted to be in it. Although we watched them as closely as possible, with just a few seconds turning our eyes away from them, the unthinkable happened. I thank God my husband was a quick responder and a great swimmer. Without hesitation, he dove into the water to save and rescue them.

It was no different in the hospital, too, for me. My boy needed protecting within and without. It's not to say that every person he met during that time was evil. And evil was lurking around every corner. Maybe that was the perception. However, the Holy Spirit was already showing me a better way to listen to his voice. I was no longer a "traditional" Christian. Traditional in a sense where I show up to church on Sunday, sing a few songs, listen to my pastor preach, say hi to a few of my fellow brothers and sisters in Christ, and go home until next week when it starts all over again. The Holy Spirit was showing me how to fight in the spirit realm. The Word of God tells us to work out our salvation with fear and trembling.

> Wherefore, my beloved, as ye have always obeyed, not as in my presence only, but now much more in my absence, work out your salvation with fear and trembling. For it is God which worketh in you both to will and to do of his good pleasure.

Philippians 2:12-13

What is this thing that we must work out? And why with fear and trembling? Sometimes, as Christians, we feel like salvation alone is a struggle. The struggle, I've discovered, is our disobedience toward what God is calling us to do. We see this clearly at the beginning of the verse when Paul mentions, "as ye have always obeyed." Our salvation sometimes, most of the time, cannot be exercised unless there is direct opposition or an action that is contrary to what the Holy Spirit has been showing us. If there wasn't, there would be no need to work out our salvation. We must take everything Jesus paid for at the cross and apply it to every situation in our lives. We need to obey God and believe His Word.

The Beginning of the Beginning

What is salvation? The theological definition is a deliverance from sin and its consequences through faith in Christ. What are the consequences of sin? Death, sickness, disease, lack, loss, and the list goes on. I pondered this for a moment one morning and thought, "Sickness falls in the same line as sin." It too had been dealt with on the cross. And it was. Jesus delivered us from sickness and disease.

Finally, for once in my life, I felt like what a true Christian should be. Where the rubber meets the road so to speak. This is what salvation truly means. I was either going to believe God and in all His promises or give in to the devil, which could mean taking my son. It was scary to walk out in boldness against all odds. I had to look past the stares, the disbelief, and the side conversations that took place and continue in God's presence in a world that cannot understand where you are coming from.

To prepare my son for the surgery, we did what we were familiar with at home; we had a small Bible study. Sometimes during the Bible studies, I wasn't sure if it made any difference in our personal lives. I never knew if anything was sinking into my son's mind and heart. If what we did was for nil, or how my son felt toward God and the events he experienced in his young life. Did he have any resentment that he wasn't aware of in his teenage years?

I say now that they did have an impact, and the enemy knows that it does. He puts up a smoke screen and minimizes everything godly, so we can focus on our problems.

None of the unanswered questions mattered in our Bible study in the hospital room. This was life and death, and I chose life. The passage of focus during that evening before surgery was in Ephesians 6:10-18:

> Finally, my brethren, be strong in the Lord and the power of His might. Put on the whole armor of God, so that you may be able to stand against the wiles of the devil. For we do not wrestle against flesh and blood, but against principalities, against powers, against the rulers of the darkness of this age, against spiritual hosts of wickedness in the heavenly places. Therefore take up the whole armor of God, that you may be able to withstand in the evil day, and having done all, to stand. Stand therefore, having girded your waist with truth, having put on the breastplate of righteousness, and having shod your feet with the preparation of the gospel of peace; above all, taking the shield of faith with which you will be able to quench all the fiery darts of the

> wicked one. And take the helmet of salvation, and the sword of the Spirit, which is the word of God; praying always with all prayer and supplication in the Spirit, being watchful to this end with all perseverance and supplication for all the saints.

I instructed my son to remember these words when he comes out from surgery. He shook his head in agreement, closed his eyes, and fell asleep. The surgery was scheduled very early in the morning, so I fell asleep, too.

The next morning, right before my son was headed to the operating room, a few of his friends and their sweet parents came and prayed over him. He was blessed with a special guest as one of his friend's aunts was an ordained minister. She prayed for a special blessing over my son, and we all agreed. In a sense, they kind of took over the place. I stood back and watched as these warriors of faith believed God in His Word and imparted their love and support to my son. If anyone was feeling just as bad as the next person, it would be his dear friends. Nonetheless, they put those feelings aside and stood by and with him to this very day.

Sometimes in life, you forget that there are people who truly care. I know their prayers were answered because everything after that began to fall into place. God puts very special people in your path at very specific times. As long as I live, I will never forget each person who stood by my son. God knows what you need even before you ask. He works through us—me and you—to accomplish His plans no matter what the enemy throws your way. We truly have nothing to worry about. We know how the story ends.

It was time for my son to head to the operating room. His friends said goodbye, and they were off to school. After they left, it was just my son and me. Then, he went past the double doors, and I had to stay in the waiting area. My son's friends, how impressive they were in their way of dealing with something like this. Watching their dear friend experience so much in life at a very young age and dealing with their struggles. Although they headed for school, it was just too tough for them to concentrate. I think about boundaries when it comes to trials. There are none. Trials come to all of us at any age. I often think of the passages in the Bible that spoke of children being sick and Jesus healing them. How earthly-minded we are as adults often. We need to heed Jesus' advice and be as children are.

You never know whom you will draw strength from. People come across your path and are here one day and gone the next. But they were in your path, and something they said or did make you think about your own life. For instance, this man worked at the same place I did at that time. He, too, was there at the hospital that morning with his wife's family. She was the one having surgery that morning.

Months later when I ran into him at work, he told me how his wife was doing. He also talked about his faith and how he and his wife were surrounded by strong warriors of faith. He got me thinking, "Am I a warrior of faith?" We talked about confessions and things we say, and people say that don't make any sense in God's kingdom. Maybe a person is sick because God wants to teach them something. Or God took someone away because He wanted another angel in Heaven. I'm not at all making fun of anyone who says these things and thinks this way. There's just no truth and faith behind these sayings. He said he knew of some women who were strong in their faith for healing. I wondered, "Would someone think of me as a person with strong faith?"

While waiting there in the lobby of the hospital, a few family members came and offered their support. I'm not sure if anyone knew what was going on or if they could feel the unsurmountable weight of the situation. Mentally, I wasn't paying attention to any conversations going on at that time. There are just some things you can't talk away with, and I wasn't up to talking much that day, so I silently prayed and thought of my son. I was blessed to see people there offering a word of encouragement. But in my mind, I wanted to get away for a while. Jesus often went off by Himself—away from his disciples and away from crowds. There is strength in the presence of the Lord.

Hours passed, and it was late in the afternoon, almost close to evening, and surgery was done. My son did great. The surgeon did great, too. And everyone who came by to demonstrate their support left, and a few came by later that evening.

Before I was allowed to see my son, I had to wait some additional time. When they called me in to see him, they wanted me to talk to him even though he was still sedated. I whispered in his ear and asked him if he remembered what we talked about the night before—about the armor of God. He nodded, yes. I whispered, "When you wake up, remember what we talked about. They will be pulling a tube from your mouth. Don't panic."

They wheeled him to his room and began prepping him for the removal of the tube. When they finally did, it was not a good sight. I will spare the details, but I panicked. They told me to leave the room and not to enter back until they gave me the okay. After a brief while, I got to see my son all settled in. Amen.

I didn't get the chance to speak to the surgeon right away. When I saw him, he looked very exhausted, and rightfully so. With encouragement from one of my son's friend's parents, I asked what he discovered. He said he didn't think he would be able to, but he completely removed the tumor. He showed me images of the brain and where he had to cut away the mass. He said it was so deep that his gag reflexes may be sensitive because the tumor was in the area that controls these senses. I was hesitant to ask, but I mentioned the spine although there was no surgery performed on the spine. He looked at the images and said, "I'm not sure what that is, but it doesn't look like cancer."

The spine. Until this day, no one could tell us what a little "spot" in my son's spine is. Before he left the hospital, a biopsy was taken of the small spot. Although I had to wait for the results for some time, I'm glad they came a little later. All in God's timing.

Chapter 5

LIFE OR DEATH

Death and life are in the power of the
tongue: and they that love it shall eat the
fruit thereof.

Proverbs 18:31

I would imagine that maybe most people would receive results right away, especially with something as se-
rious as a brain tumor. Truth is, we didn't get results right
away. We had to leave the city to find out what my son
had. I'll talk about that in another chapter. From what I
was told, there had to be three pathologists to confirm what
the tumor was—what type of cancer. One pathologist said
one thing, another said something different, and the other
wasn't sure. For at least a month, we still had no official
diagnosis. And because of this, and for many other legiti-
mate reasons, no one was allowed to speak of cancer in the
presence of my son.

It all started with a visit from an oncologist a day after
my son's operation, one I didn't know and recognized. He
walked into my son's room and began to ask him how he
felt and how he felt about having a tumor. What an odd

question, I thought. No one would be excited about that. But I think he wanted to know how he felt about having cancer.

Because my son was still exhausted from the surgery he walked over and started talking to me. He was interested in having my son as one of his patients. I told him we still didn't have a diagnosis and were unsure how we would proceed. He said he was almost positive about what it was. He told me if I didn't pursue treatment his chances of survival would be slim, and if I did, he also gave me those statistics. I told him, "I'm not ready to make any decisions now." The doctor also mentioned my son possibly going through trials so the results from that could help other children in similar situations. He said that if one of his children had what my son had, he would have them go through these trial treatments. How strange, I thought— that a doctor would speak of such things, confess these things about his children.

Well, that statement pretty much did it for me. I escorted the doctor out, and I asked the staff not to allow him back into my son's room and that I didn't want him around my son at all. I was not interested in my son being an example, and I know why he was interested. Very few children in the US get this type of disease. It's rare. I'm not sure of the percentage, but roughly a little over a thousand children each year get this disease.

I did not intend to be rude to the doctor by any means. However, negativity in my son's room and life was not accepted. No one was allowed to talk about cancer around my son and me. To some, this may seem harsh and uncaring; however, I needed to maintain focus, think about things clearly, and stay sensitive to God's voice. The decision was mine alone, along with what I knew God was telling me to do. He worked with me where I was. And I know if I'm doing what God is telling me to do, then his approval is what matters.

The immediate hospital staff was unhappy with my decision about what could be discussed around my son. Word went around even to those not directly involved with his recovery. I remember one occasion when a hospital staff member came to my son's room and asked to speak to me about my insurance coverage. We both stood outside the door to my son's room, and she confessed that she wasn't there to go over insurance because she didn't work with insurance at all. The main reason she was there was to ask why I didn't want to talk to my son about cancer and why the hospital staff was not allowed to speak of it in his presence. I did not appreciate the deceit, and without hesitation and with complete steadfastness, I told her it was my decision and that my convictions should be respected. Stunned by my answer, she accepted my reason – for a while.

Later, the same person convinced another staff member to invite me and my son to a room filled with games, books, and movies. We decided to go to give my son a change in scenery. The staff member had recently been over to this person's house to console her over the death of her cat. While we were there, the two of them tried to convince me and my son that death is a beautiful thing.

Satan tried everything he could to get me to back down. Even doctors had a "talk" with me and asked the same questions other hospital personnel did. And my answer remained the same throughout the entire time my son was there. Eventually, the hospital staff reluctantly complied, and life went on. I was not about to confess anything to my son, nor was I going to allow anyone else to pronounce any sickness, disease, or death on him, knowingly or unknowingly.

When you choose to walk this life by following biblical principles and the leading of the Holy Spirit, you will get pushback. Some may not understand your decisions because we have been taught to live by our feelings and emotions. I declare that my son is alive and well today because I said no to the devil and chose not to believe the negative words, lies, and deceit. God has already provided the answer for our healing and life. It's our responsibility to act on his promises and not negate them with our negative words, thoughts, and actions. Better yet, the contrary thoughts and actions of others, too.

> I call heaven and earth to record this day against you, *that* I have set before you life and death, blessing and cursing: therefore choose life, that both thou and thy seed may live:" "That thou mayest love the LORD thy God, *and* that thou mayest obey his voice, and that thou mayest cleave unto him: for he *is* thy life, and the length of thy days: that thou mayest dwell in the land which the LORD swore unto thy fathers, to Abraham, to Isaac, and to Jacob, to give them.

Deuteronomy 30:19-20

Chapter 6

LOVE OF A FATHER AND MOTHER

Children, obey your parents in the Lord: for this is right. Honour thy father and mother; which is the first commandment with promise; That it may be well with thee, and thou mayest live long on the earth.

Ephesians 6:1-3

After three weeks in the hospital, my son was finally released. He was very tired of being in there and wanted to go home. Unfortunately, it was not going to be that easy. At that point, my son needed constant care, and I still needed to work. I asked my parents if it was okay for us to move into their home for a while, just until things became a little more settled in my next steps with my son. They agreed. About a week before we had some idea as to when he would be released, we started moving a few items from our home and taking them to my parents' home.

Living with my parents was a blessing. My mom became my son's caregiver while I went to work. It was quite a task because my son dealt with constant nausea and

47

vomiting, and many times did not feel like eating. At the hospital, he had a feeding tube stuck down his throat, and that didn't work and made him feel terrible. Then, he had a feeding tube in his navel area, and that stayed there for a while. This seemed, at that time, the only way he could get some sustenance. Because it was difficult to hold down food, we had to resort to giving him liquid food through that tube. So, leaving my son for the entire day was hard, but I know he was in good hands with my parents. My mom would be concerned about his not eating. And to tell you the truth, this would concern anyone. But she tried to encourage him to eat and monitor the feeding contraption.

The last thing I wanted to do was to be a burden to my parents. It appeared in my life that trouble and heart-ache tended to follow our family. And I know it was hard for them to watch us go through something else again. But there was nothing I could do but rely on God and he was providing the way for my son's healing and getting us all through this time. And I was still growing into the mature Christian God always wanted me to be. All these things seemed to be coming together all at the same time. When I finally settled into my parents' home, things began to weigh very heavily on me. I know it was hard being around me, and I can see why people would stay away. I couldn't explain it, nor could I ask anyone to understand.

It seemed like everything was coming down hard, even at work. And so, the compilation of everything got to me a few times. Although I tried to hide my feelings to keep some normalcy in their home, you just can't hide things from your parents. They did their best to make us feel right at home. We were not able to fully grasp the blessing that my parents gave us then, because it centered around my son getting well. It's not something we anticipated doing, and we missed our home.

My mom and I are like a team. She went with us everywhere, even stayed with us in the hospital room and even out of town. So, she was very familiar with doctors' appointments and how they went. And when we were staying there, she was the one who would take my son to his appointments while I was at work. I gave her strict orders not to listen to the doctors' negative feedback, the nursing staff, or whomever he would see that day. Sometimes, she would send me a message to let me know what they were discussing, I'd respond by saying," In Jesus' name," to answer that question. Or don't believe the lies. On one occasion, my mom or my son asked me a question through a message about a concern the medical staff had, and they needed feedback. My replies were very much the same. After a while, they asked what my response was. They answered by saying I was binding and rebuking the negative words. I think the hospital staff got a kick out of that, but it was the truth. The fact is, the fight, if you will, was not with the medical staff; it was against the demonic forces that kept trying to place obstacles in my son's way to get him to think that God doesn't heal. Now, we may say in our minds and express with our mouths that that's not what we believe or that's not what we say. The reality is, for most of us, it wouldn't take much for us to think contrary to what the word of God says. At least this goes for me.

There was no question about how I felt about healing. And the medical staff knew it. I think they preferred my mother over me at those appointments. In either case, I couldn't let my guard down, even if I wasn't present. She represented me, and we represented Christ. I don't know what we would have done without her.

I still remember the night we stayed in a hotel in a near-by city when it still wasn't clear to me where all this was going. Should my son receive treatment? What would they discover? Many other questions plagued me. I know my mom was scared, too. Anyway, we settled in for the night and while we were trying to get some sleep, I asked my mom basically what we were to do. She quoted a scripture to me that I never heard, but I read it. It meant so much to me to hear it coming from her. It brought me much comfort. She brought me much comfort.

> When thou passest through the waters, I will be with thee; and through the rivers, they shall not overflow thee: when thou walkest through the fire, thou shalt not be burned; neither shall the flame kindle upon thee.

Isaiah 43:2

When we stayed a while at that nearby City my mom stayed with us there. I know being in those appointments was mentally draining, to say the least. But my mom remained tough. Because I wanted to engulf myself in God's Word for many reasons, she followed. We had plenty of Christian books to read, and when I finished one, she began to read it. One day, after coming back from the grocery store, she looked at me and said she was ready to move deeper with God. I'm paraphrasing her words, but she was quoting a passage in this book that references getting on board with God. I knew what she meant. She had to lay down all the fears, worries, and anxiety she felt and started and begin a life dedicated to trusting God's promises, no matter what. That was one of the best things I had heard.

Because my parents got me to a point where I could take care of my son without so much assistance, I found a place close to his school to live for a few years. Living with them was the best choice I made. In retrospect, the months went by quickly. At least for me, they did. My son, perhaps at the time, may have seen his grandmother as someone who was just trying to get him to eat, but I know to this day, he appreciates all she did for him.

Chapter 7

WHAT THE NAKED EYE CAN'T SEE

And they came to Jericho: and as he went out of Jericho with his disciples and a great number of people, blind Bartimaeus, the son of Timaeus, sat by the highway side begging. And when he heard that it was Jesus of Nazareth, he began to cry out, and say, Jesus, *thou* Son of David, have mercy on me. And many charged him that he should hold his peace: but he cried the more a great deal, *Thou* Son of David, have mercy on me. And Jesus stood still and commanded him to be called. And they call the blind man, saying unto him, Be of good comfort, rise; he calleth thee. And he, casting away his garment, rose, and came to Jesus. And Jesus answered and said unto him, What wilt thou that I should do unto thee? The blind man said unto him, Lord, that I might receive my sight. And Jesus said unto him, "Go thy way; thy faith hath made thee whole. And immediately he received his sight and followed Jesus in the way."

Mark 10:46-52

I can remember many times being so scared that I could hardly function. It's as if I was paralyzed, literally paralyzed. The reason I felt this way was because I kept focusing on the natural things—things that were right in front of me that for the most part didn't look too good. But that was just the enemy creating a screen of terror that I couldn't see past it. I John 4:17 tells us: "There is no fear in love, but perfect love casteth out fear: because fear hath torment."

Fear blinds you to the truth. It prevents you from receiving from the Lord. The first time I became aware of this fear was a few weeks after my son had surgery and needed another scan. When he entered the room where the scans take place, the nurse became so surprised and wondered if it was the same patient that had just gone through surgery weeks ago.

She said he looked great and was happy to see him doing well. I was shocked. Was I missing something? Because the boy I see could hardly keep food down, he had a tube that ran down his throat and was being fed that way temporarily. He could walk but had a balance issue. He looked depressed and understandably so. How can a person look at him and say he looks great?

On another occasion, while living with my parents, he

became so sick that my dad and I had to take him to the emergency room. We were not sure of what was going on with him: was it intestinal, or was it his head that he was feeling bad about? I wasn't quite sure, but he needed medical care. While sitting there waiting for some answers, the ER doctor walks in and says to him, "How are you feeling?" my son responds to his question. Then the doctor, with a big smile, goes on to say to him, "By the way, I just want to say you look great." My inward reaction was dumbfounded, and my thoughts were, *"Can't you see that he's not doing well? He's lost quite a bit of weight from vomiting so much."* I couldn't believe what I was hearing.

The natural world, where we operate most of the time, is the area we see with our eyes. However, we need to move past that and into the spiritual realm, like Jesus was when healing the sick. He saw them well. He knew the promises and operated in them by coming alongside and agreeing with their faith (verse 52). I can almost see Jesus now when healing the sick. He didn't dismiss them and say, "You're not sick." Nor did He say they were imagining their sickness. No, He met them where they were and healed them.

The same goes for us, too. What do we have to lose, trusting in the Lord? It was obvious that my son was sick, but it wasn't obvious to me, yet that Jesus had already healed him. I focused on the wrong thing and let fear get the best of me. I needed to see in the Spirit all of God's promises playing out in my son's life regardless of how he looked and felt. And, yes, regardless of what someone might think otherwise.

In verse 51 above, Jesus asked blind Bartimaeus what he would like him to do for him. I had not seen this before, but Bartimaeus didn't ask Jesus to heal his eyes, he asked him if he could help him *receive* his sight. He already knew Jesus healed, but maybe he was having difficulty receiving that healing. I believe when he cast away his garments in verse 50, he was casting away doubts and unbelief. And when he came to Jesus, the question was not about healing but rather, about receiving. Once Bartimaeus confessed to Jesus what he truly wanted and needed to see, Jesus confirmed his request by expressing to him that his faith, (and his cast-off unbelief) had made him whole. That's all Bartimaeus needed to hear, and immediately he *received* his sight.

I needed to start walking in healing, too, if I wanted my son to receive the same. That meant I had to cast off unbelief and fear. If my son saw me frightened, he too became frightened. Once I realized that I wasn't seeing with my Spiritual eyes, my whole view of seeing things became clearer and clearer. We walk by faith and not by sight (II Corinthians 5:7). Like blind Bartimaeus, I had to ask Jesus to help me *receive* my sight.

To help me better understand receiving healing, I began researching all the scriptures on healing from the Gospels. In each book, Matthew, Mark, Luke, and John there are accounts of healing. I began to count the number of times healing took place in each book and how. I remember one night while getting ready for bed, I was almost done with the book of Luke in counting the number of times healing took place and was mentioned. When praying, I raised a question to God. I wondered why the book of Luke has more accounts of healing than the others. I left it at that and went to bed. I didn't give God a chance to answer the question.

When I woke up in the morning, I'll never forget the first thing God spoke to me, "Luke was a physician." Wow! Of course! Luke was interested in anything having to do with the human body because that was his profession. The kind of healing that came from God probably interested him because it didn't rely on medicine for that period. He would be the one God chose to write this book and mention more healing accounts because he had an understanding in that area. Luke *received* God's healing power.

How much more did I need to do the same? To follow the accounts of healing and make them my own. It's not an impossible thing for Jesus to heal someone. It's not impossible because He already paid the price on the cross. Healing comes from God. I can see from the Word of God that His divine plan for humanity from the beginning was to be in good and perfect health. He wants us to be well today. I believe the words of healing need to get out of the pages of the Bible and into our hearts to *receive* them. We have work to do. We need to fulfill God's purpose in our lives. Anything less than God's best keeps us from walking in God's will for our lives. If we only see sickness and let fear overtake us, then we can't move forward with His plan. It's important to keep our minds focused on God and His Word so that we don't have problems *receiving* and we can see what is happening in the spiritual realm.

Chapter 8

THE DEVIL IS DEFEATED AND JESUS TRIUMPHS

And he said unto them, I beheld Satan as lightning fall from heaven.

Luke 10:18

By this time, my son had already met with a doctor. She went over all the possibilities and what would be the best course of action. Because there was not a true diagnosis even at that point, I remembered what a parent mentioned to me while visiting my son at the hospital. She spoke of specialized medical resources in another city. I kept that advice in my heart.

After hearing the doctor talk about treatments and such, I made up my mind right then and there, where my son would get the best care. Even though the doctor had suggested we meet with a specific physician in town, my thoughts were elsewhere. Still, an appointment was made to at least speak with the physician. I debated whether to take my son to another appointment because he was weak. Even up to that day, I didn't want to take him but decided to for some reason.

When we arrived at the doctor's office, we waited a while until we were called back. After the nurse took my son's weight and temperature, she told us we would not see the doctor immediately because he was tied up in a meeting, and another doctor would meet with us until he arrived. So, we sat in the corner of the office and waited. My son was not feeling well at all, and I even think he fell asleep sitting in the chair.

The doctor walks in after a few minutes, and she begins to introduce herself. The room was quite large and not as small as some of them are, with the doctor on one end and us on the other. She starts by explaining what this certain treatment is and what the side effects would be should we choose to use that option. When she was describing the horrible things that could happen with this treatment, maybe she saw my reactions. I don't think I had a reaction on my face but was probably visualizing or rehearsing the complete opposite in my mind. Her words went in one ear and out the other because I refused to accept them. I didn't allow them to stay in the atmosphere as I was rebuking inside of me every single negative word. The words were full of death, and I was not in agreement with death but chose life. Maybe she thought I wasn't paying attention, but I was. I was not receiving those words for my son. Nor for myself.

The Devil is Defeated and Jesus Triumphs

After she ended, I asked her, "Are these things some-one could get or will get?" She rolled her stool on wheels over to me and said, "He will get them." Just then, the door opened, and I heard a vague male voice talking to the doctor. I couldn't hear what was being said, nor could I see the person because there was a curtain blocking our view. Then the doctor said she would be back and out the door, she went. As I sat there, I could feel no fear. My son was half asleep next to me, and I'm not even sure he would remember anything she said. Which is a good thing.

After a moment, a male person walks in. It's the doctor whom we were there to see initially. He introduced him-self and while wringing his hands with hand sanitizer, told us, "Well, the results from the spine are in, and there is no cancer. That's good news."

It took a doctor from a different field to give me results from a test taken over a month ago at another facility. It was not by some chance that the Lord impressed on my heart to go to this appointment. He also started to tell me that my son could live a fulfilled life. That he knows an adult person, who had the same thing my son may have and is living a very successful life. He was very optimistic, unlike the doctor before him, and all-around positive.

Satan tried to steal not only my son's life away, but

every piece of hope and faith we had. He used the doctor to try and scare us to make us think that there was no way my son would ever have any chance in life. But God has other plans. He says no one can pluck us out of his hands.

> My sheep hear my voice, and I know them, and they follow me: And I give unto them eternal life, and they shall never perish, neither shall any man pluck them out of my hand.

John 10:27-28

I'm so glad we made that appointment. I would not have heard the good news that my son's spine was okay and cancer-free. We may have missed hearing the positive feedback that he can lead a fulfilled life. Not that we needed confirmation on that. It was good to hear. Above all, I saw Satan defeated that day. When he tried to kick us when we were down, Jesus came and lifted us. Hallelujah!

Chapter 9

COMING TO THE SECRET PLACE

He that dwelleth in the secret place of the
most High shall abide under the shadow
of the Almighty.

Psalm 91:1

Although I knew we had to leave the city to get the best medical care my son could receive, I had no idea how we were going to get there. No one will ever understand the complete and utter struggle it was to keep my son alive. No one ever will. But through the struggle, God placed helpful people in our path. The outpour we received was immeasurable. I still feel overwhelmed by love even to this very day. One of the people God put in our path to get us to the next step was a sweet parent who was all too familiar with dealing with an illness herself.

When the parent contacted me, she wanted me to know that she respected my wishes and was in no way trying to get me to do something I did not want to do. I'm so glad she respected that part about me. I didn't want to reveal too much to everyone because I knew what my son was going through was very difficult for some to grasp. We needed strong individuals at this point.

She also said I didn't have to reveal anything I didn't want to anyone. It is no one's business what we are going through, and I don't have to tell everyone the story. I was so happy to hear that. I'm a quiet person and to keep telling the story of what my son was going through seemed like it was being re-lived repeatedly.

We set up a time to call the out-of-town medical center I had been thinking of to prepare for our first visit. Then we met at a place to send off the information they requested. While we waited for assistance, she spoke to me about her healing journey. I still remember the photographs she shared that represented life, freed from sickness and disease, somehow telling the enemy, "I'm still here!" She may not have realized that what she was doing was bringing hope and encouragement. She contacted me a few days before we were scheduled to leave and made me a binder to keep track of all the meetings we would have with the physicians.

What I appreciated about this dear, sweet parent was how she helped me get my mind off things. All she did was with great care, respecting my wishes without wanting anything from me. It's not that I couldn't give; I didn't have the energy to. I was being attacked from all sides at that time. It wasn't just my son's health I was dealing with. Nonetheless, I kept going even though I couldn't see the day ahead of me. I took small steps a little at a time, not necessarily knowing where they would lead, and God put everything into place.

Deciding on medical care in another city was one thing; we also needed to find a place to stay temporarily while visiting. When we spoke with someone from the medical center, I was sent instructions and a list of affordable places we could stay. During my breaks at work, I'd go down the list and make a few calls. Some of these places were at capacity; another was under construction. None of them were working out except one.

After calling so many places, I guess the person on the other end of the line could probably sense the frustration in my voice. Asking if there was availability was tough. I didn't want to hear another rejection, but I needed to know. When I called this one last place, it was not easy to get an answer as to whether there was room for my son, me, and my mom. But I continued to inquire anyway. After answering a few questions, the gentleman suggested a small apartment that would suit us well for the time we needed. I mentioned to him that we would probably be arriving in the evening of said day. He said he didn't mind waiting.

With a confirmed place to stay and a deep breath, we all packed for a long stay. I had no idea where this place was located exactly or what it looked like, but I had an address. Off we went on a three-and-a-half-hour drive. After many turns and missed exits, we finally found the place. It was tucked between what looked like the beginnings of new apartments and the other a well-established residential area. However, I smiled while driving through the small parking lot. You see, this was no ordinary building—it resembled a temple.

Walking inside this place was awe-inspiring. There was no one at the front desk, but eventually, a lady came and assisted. I mentioned to her that a gentleman was expecting us. She called and spoke to a man on the phone in a foreign language. Still, I had no idea what this place was, but I found out quickly.

The lady told me someone would be here shortly. I waited a few minutes, and in came a man who appeared to be a Rabbi. He wore black, was wearing a kippa, and had a long beard. Well, he looked like a Rabbi. I signed a few documents. Made a deposit. He explained a few things and provided me with a parking sticker that I still have on my windshield to this very day. I went back to my vehicle and got our things and we settled into our temporary apartment. It was a very modern space, well taken care of, and everything was high-end.

After we decided who would sleep where and put all our things away, I told my mom that I would be touring the place, beginning on our floor. Right by the elevator just on the other side where the apartments were, there was another space dedicated to small gatherings or meetings, a play area for kids, a kitchen, a seating area, and a patio. Then I went downstairs to a section opposite the main lobby where I found a space for large gatherings, and right next to it was the main kitchen. To the left of that room was the synagogue. Heading toward the front entrance, off to the right, are two living spaces. In front of that, in a small corner, is a place where guests can enjoy coffee and soup.

There's a side entrance to the building. When you walk out – you're walking into a small garden area with a very large wall water feature. It's a space where you can sit and meditate and enjoy the scenery. To the right of the garden area, there is a pathway that will take you to the herb garden and flower gardens. I was so happy to see that. I love gardening and eventually, I'd make my contribution to this extended sanctuary.

After about an hour or so, I went back to the apartment.

We made dinner and within a few hours, we went to bed because my son would see quite a few doctors the following day. And at one of those appointments, I was hoping to find more answers.

The next few days, my son had appointments from sun-up to sundown, Monday through Friday. On the weekends, we drove back home when we could and stayed a few nights, and come Sunday afternoon, we headed back. My mom and my son didn't like returning, but I didn't mind, because that's when I knew I could meet God without interruptions. And I needed to prepare myself spiritually for the days, weeks, months, and years ahead.

After about a week and a half stay, and appointments just the same, one day, we finally received an explanation of what my son had. The doctor and the nurse practitioner escorted us to a room with an actual door, not the sliding one, this one had a knob. The door closed behind us, and the doctor began to tell us what they discovered based on the scans that were sent to them before our arrival. After listening to the "diagnosis," something within me welled up. I began to argue the case that the pathologists back home did not all agree. And the same thing goes for the spine. The doctor listened and said whether my son gets better, or it turns out to be something else, the diagnosis will remain the same, it will not change. I told him to interpret the pathology notes for the spine. I said, there it states that he does not have cancer in the spine. He either didn't have them in front of him, or he was not going to refer to them.

I left very disappointed and angry. Angry because I knew better. But there was no way my son was at the stage the pathologist at this place said he was. It didn't matter what I thought in many ways. The doctor was not going to change his mind. And really, God has the last say. He has our days numbered, not the doctors, not a diagnosis, not what anyone else says, but God. I needed to settle this part in my mind no matter what was said to me and my son.

Before leaving for my stay in this city, I was seeking the Lord on these things, doing everything I could to avoid negative comments or feedback, and stares of disbelief. I stayed far away and kept people at a distance if they weren't in agreement with God's Word. Every day, I would pour my heart out on God's Word and search it for hidden treasures. And being in this new place was no different.

Very early in the morning, around three, I'd sneak out of the apartment and take with me a napkin I had written on, a writing pen, and a Hebrew Bible I borrowed, and sit by the small library next to the kitchenette. And that's where I would spend my mornings, seeking God, reading the Bible, and praying. At first, I didn't know where to start reading. The Bible I borrowed started backward with the books. With Genesis at the end. The Holy Spirit would guide me through the Bible – what to read. And then one morning, I was directed to a very special place in His Word. This was my answer.

On another occasion, after one of his appointments, I turned on the television to see if I could catch someone ministering God's Word. I came to like the Rabbi that would come out about noon. He would close his message with a blessing, and I liked that. Then right after, I would listen intently to a soft-spoken man, sitting at a table, ministering God's truth as I'd never heard. I had heard and noticed him years prior. It was at that moment, if not in the past, I knew we could get through this because we already had the victory. Jesus has already paid the price. I didn't have to beg God to help us like I did when my husband was in his last days. I would go into a chapel at this one place he was at, and I would lay prostrate on the carpeted floor and beg God for a miracle. God doesn't work this way. And He's not a mystery. In His Word are promises. It's up to us to live them out in complete faith and belief. We can't wait for something to happen and then pray a "shotgun" prayer, and everything is going to be all right.

It's what you do in the meantime, day after day, week after week, and year after year that builds your faith to fight the enemy when things come your way.

I didn't realize it, but there was a magazine in this waiting area where my son needed a scan. It was a Christian one, and there was a story of a man who was praying for a child to live. He and the child's family were praying for this boy's complete recovery. But the boy passed away. The pastor couldn't figure it out. He had faith; he knew God healed. Later, after speaking with the child's mother, she confessed to doubting her son's healing. This story spoke to me. Months later, I realized that the man in this story is the same man I was listening to that one afternoon who stirred up my faith that God wants my son well and we already have all we need because of what Jesus paid for at the cross.

Days after the diagnosis, we hadn't seen the doctor for a few appointments. I'm not sure why. But at one of these visits, it started as they usually do, with the nurse asking my son a series of questions, going over medications, and testing his balance. Then a visitor came by and talked to us about assistance and education. While my son was talking to the nurse and I listening to the visitor, the doctor walked in with his assistant. They didn't come further than the door, and the doctor stood there smiling. He looked at me and said, "You were right. There is no cancer in the spine." He stayed there for a minute nodding his head in agreement with the same smile on his face, and then they both walked out. I turned to my mom and, "God answers prayer." Amen!

To get to that place, I had to start focusing on how I saw my son in the future. I had to see him walk the stage at his high school graduation. I saw him going to college. I saw him with a family even though the doctors said he could be sterile from therapy. It wasn't easy at times, because when you're in a hospital setting, doom and gloom surround it just about all the time. You're fighting non-believers; you're fighting in the spiritual world. To try and be positive in that environment, people look at you funny like you're crazy. They are not in agreement with the Holy Spirit as you are. It's truly a fight for life in every way.

Every day and every week we were there, I kept pressing into the Lord. Even after I got back from spending time with the Lord off to the side of the kitchenette, it was hard to fall asleep. All kinds of thoughts would flood my mind. On nights when I couldn't fall asleep right away, I'd turn on the TV to a Christian station that played soft music to images of landscape scenes. And after a few minutes, Bible verses appeared in the foreground, fading in and out.

Visiting a big city can be a bit overwhelming. Living in one for over a month is even more so. To be quite honest, I liked this place. It was home away from home. I can remember every detail about it even today. I felt very at peace there. Maybe because it was to me like coming into God's throne room.

Chapter 10

COMING TO THE SECRET PLACE CONTINUED AND PSALM 91

Surely he shall deliver thee from the snare of the fowler, and the noisome pestilence. He shall cover thee with his feathers, and under his wings shalt thou trust: his truth shall be thy shield and buckler. Thou shall not be afraid for the terror by night; nor for the destruction that wasteth at noonday. A thousand shall fall at thy right hand, but it shall not come nigh thee.

Psalm 91: 3-7

I still remember those times as if they were yesterday; waking up early in the morning, being as quiet as I could be out of respect for the other patients staying in the same complex and floor, not knowing exactly what God would say to me until one morning the Holy Spirit directed me to Psalm 91.

At first, I read through the whole chapter, as I had in the past; not fully paying attention to the verses and seeing how they can be applied to my life. I needed to do something that I had not done since my early twenties; delve wholeheartedly into God's word. Honestly, I desired to have the Word engulf me. I just didn't know how to get there again. And at the end of the day, hearing about sickness and seeing it all around us, I couldn't wait to get back to the apartment.

As excited as I was to meet with God at the small library, there were days I felt discouraged that I could hardly read. Nevertheless, after a good cry, I'd open the Bible to Psalm 91. One morning, instead of just reading the verses word for word, I began to insert my son's name in them. This was new to me. In the past, I'd known God was speaking to me through his word, but I never made it personal to insert my name in any verse or someone else's name to take it even further. For example, verse 7 of this Psalm, reads: "A thousand shall fall at thy side, and ten thousand at thy right hand, but it shall not come nigh thee." I would then say, "This disease shall not come nigh my son."

In this psalm, it struck me how God chose his words carefully to describe in detail what he is trying to communicate to us. He used names of his creations and perhaps uncommon professions to hone our thoughts and imaginations, so they penetrated our hearts. When God gave us His word, he made it so that no matter where anyone is in life, it will apply to you. He already provided all the answers we need in life through His Word. However, we must seek to find the answers. It's not something we will automatically have common knowledge about. It's up to us to find out what God says about our situation and our future.

> For I know the thoughts that I think to-ward you, saith the LORD, thoughts of peace, and not of evil, to give you an ex-pected end. Then shall ye call upon me, and ye shall go and pray unto me, and I will hearken unto you.

Jeremiah 29:11-12

No one could have expressed, to a large degree, the utter importance of seeking God than King David. You can sense his agony and his deep desire to be with God in this psalm and others written by him. However, this chapter not only gives insight into how David viewed and trusted God; it provides us with the truth about who God is and what we have in knowing Him. The revelation into who God is begins in verse 1 of this psalm. While some may focus on dwelling in a secret place, what caught my attention is where this place is; it's under the shadow of the Almighty. And under His shadow is where we stay or abide. It's a shadow because His presence is vast; it can engulf and house many. There is no limit. That's how great God is!

The second verse reveals what the psalmist was thinking and more importantly knew. Someone who has experienced dwelling in a secret place can say God is their refuge and fortress. Refuge when you're feeling down or going through something that only God can help you with. He is that place you can go to and be and feel safe. And a fortress to protect you from the world's entanglements, views, opinions, lack of faith, lack of belief, and everything contrary to God's nature—who He is.

The third verse. What a verse. It begins with the word Surely. *"Surely he shall deliver thee from the snare of the fowler, and the noisome pestilence."* To me, this word means, there is no question. No need to worry. If God said it, then it's going to happen. The word "fowler" is one of those words, too, where God uses this example to further the point of what He is communicating. A fowler is someone who hunts birds, and the snare is the trap that is set to capture birds. It's not a coincidence that verse 4 of this same chapter mentions feathers and wings. God knows there are traps in our path, and when we fall into them, He promises deliverance.

In the latter part of verse 3, the psalmist did not fail in covering all bases, both the physical things we can see with our eyes, such as a trap, and the things we cannot see, only their manifestation, such as a pestilence. No matter the situation, we must confess, as he did, to whom we trust. By living in God's presence, we are safe from fearful events, occurrences, and the like bringing harm to us.

Some mornings when my heart was heavy, I'd take the Bible in my arm, fall on my knees, and then lay prostrate on the cold white tiled floor and cry unto God. To this day, I cannot remember exactly what I would talk to him about. Most of the time, there was silence as I thought about how awesome He is and that He deserves my respect and silence. Other times, of course, I'd talk to him about what my son was going through as if he didn't know, and I would ask him to intervene. For the most part, those times were primarily focused on getting to know him in a much deeper way and letting him know I loved him no matter what. It was a time of taking what I read and learned and applying it to my life.

Every day, I was growing stronger as a Christian. And every day, my son grew stronger physically. My times with the Lord in the mornings were increasingly peaceful, and I began to look at things differently, with more assurance than before. I felt confident that it was okay to move about the place we were staying, so I began to explore it further.

Right by the small kitchenette were a few doors. I wasn't sure where they led and never thought to open them. Out of curiosity, I did. One door led to a facilities room, the other was to a room I cannot remember, and the one in the center led to the upstairs of the synagogue. All this time, right in front of me where I sat every morning, was another entrance to the sanctuary. What a find!

When I entered, immediately to the right was a wall-to-wall bookcase full of Jewish literature and used Tanakh's. Below was the first level of the sanctuary and in the center of the room, was a square-shaped podium, and there sat a large Torah. I've read that the balcony may be used by the women as Orthodox Jews separate the men and the women or maybe it's just the balcony. Whatever it was used for then, but now it became the place where I would meet God during the remaining part of our stay. It felt inviting, just like a sanctuary should be. You see, Psalm 91 was the catalyst to usher me into a deeper more meaningful relationship with God. It helped me grow stronger until I was at a point to move out—to walk through the door God had for me, and into His holy place. The space may be different, but He's always where His children gather—waiting for us to meet Him. He's never left me, and He never will. He's been good to me all my days, even from my youth.

The balcony was L-shaped. Right in front of the bookcase were rows of seats—all attached and the ones where you need to fold down the seat, and once you get up the seat automatically folds up. On the other side, toward the wide picture window were more rows of seats. On this side, you could see some of the city lights and people coming back from a long stay at the hospital. Sometimes, it would be in the wee hours of the morning.

My favorite spot where I met God and where I did most of my writing in a journal I had, was the last row just right in front of the bookcase, the last chair to the left. This is the place I would look up all the scriptures about every area of my son's life. And it was also the place where I continued to talk with God and meditate on his word thoroughly.

I found another entrance to this space. All this time, it was staring me right in the face. On the same level as our apartment was, just down the hall, there is a door—the other door that leads to the balcony. What a discovery! I didn't have to go around to the kitchenette area to get there now.

The week before our last day there, I met with God in the patio area next to the kitchenette. It was a very significant morning, as they all were, But I needed to clarify a few things this time. I started expressing everything I had been doing so far: reading, praying, fasting, and sacrificing things that were important to me. Now, I know no one can work their way to God. And he didn't ask me to do what I just mentioned. I wanted him to know I did this because I love him. And I believe his word – that He promised to care for the widows and the fatherless. So, I brought this to his attention.

I spoke with him about what he promised in his word – to take care of me and my sons. I'd say "God, your word says," and quote a scripture. I said, "I didn't write those words; you wrote them." This went on for a while – me talking and God listening. He was silent the whole time, but I knew he was there. His word tells us,

> Come now, and let us reason together,
> saith the LORD: though your sins be as
> scarlet, they shall be as white as snow;
> though they are red like crimson, they
> shall be as wool."

Isaiah 1:18

When the day came for us to leave, I remember the Rabbi and his wife sitting in the foyer area. That was my first time seeing them sit anywhere. They worked tirelessly to provide the best care for the residents. I thanked them for all they did: managing the place, cooking for patients, visiting the sick, being there for patients who didn't have anyone with them while going through treatment, and opening Shabbat to us all, no matter your faith. These are just some of the works I observed. I'm positive they did much more.

This place brought so much healing to me and my son. It was an experience I'll never forget. The positive effects of this stay are still working on us today.

Chapter 11

PHONE LINES AND CHURCH

I sought the LORD, and he heard me and
delivered me from all my fears.

Psalm 34:4

One of the things that helped tremendously during this
time was to reach out to the Christian community. Ministries have invested time and money into what are known as
prayer phone lines. The phone line minister helps anyone
who calls with a specific concern. They will listen earnest-
ly and pray according to God's word.

I remember one morning when I could not fall asleep
just thinking about the day and what was ahead. I decided
to call a prayer line. To this day, I can still recall specific
parts of the prayer the lady who answered spoke. What
she mentioned was significant and what I needed at that
moment. After all these years, I will still call prayer lines.

Perhaps prayer is a question some may have. Does
prayer work? When I pray, does God hear me? Defining
what prayer is helps us understand what happens after.
Prayer is talking to God. Jesus provided us with a prayer

structure for what they should include (Matthew 6:9–13). Prayer is also an agreement with others of like mind who stand with you for a specific need based on the Word of God (Matthew 18:19–20). Sometimes, an answer to prayer is immediate. Other times, it may take a while for it to arrive. It is not that God is not listening; other factors delay answers, but God always supplies because he is faithful (Daniel 9–10).

In a crisis, it is hard to maintain concentration. At times, many circumstances come all at once, and finding a place to be alone or to reflect on what God's Word says can be difficult. To help someone get to the next step, church ministries play a key role. With the assistance of our brothers and sisters in Christ, we can look to the future with promise.

Many friends from church were vital to my son's healing in different capacities. The pastor and his entire family let us know they were standing with us. The youth pastors often made themselves available to be by his side. During his stay in the hospital, a lady spent the night with us. We talked until daybreak without a wink of sleep. Other members kept in constant touch, letting us know we were in their prayers.

I know today that the church has come under scrutiny,

and many people may not see a need to attend or become members. I've been in church all my life; I can't imagine going through it without my Christian family. This is not a judgment on anyone who has never attended or ceased attending. Although the Christian church is not perfect, it is life-sustaining and filled with many people who love the Lord.

Conclusion

During this time, my reactions to situations, which were much more than mentioned in this book, came from knowing how God wanted me to respond to them. I didn't know what was coming against us on a day-to-day basis, but I knew that I couldn't let my guard down for one second.

I'm reminded of Matthew 4:1–11, where Jesus fasted for 40 days and was tempted by the devil. I must add that I am not at all saying I can fully understand what he went through. I'm pointing out that if Jesus needed to remind Satan who he was and who he obeys, how much more do we need to do the same? You cannot win battles by staying silent. Throughout the Bible, there are plenty of examples of someone taking some action against the enemy. We must do something; it's not just up to God. We need to speak to the mountain and command it to move. And if we're asking, or rather begging, God to move the mountains in our lives, He has already provided us with His Son; He has given us His Word. Jesus has already paid the ultimate price.

It's not about saving a life for life's sake; it's about seeing the other person live out God's plan. And when we look at our loved ones and people who have come across our path, each has a purpose—God's purpose. Jesus knew the importance and willingly went to the cross so we could live a fulfilled life here in this world and for all eternity. How we react to alarming events does have a negative or positive effect on how others respond to them. We must be the light when others see no way out, and we cannot back down, no matter what. Jesus is cheering us on. God is glorified when we use His Word to fight and win battles. Amen!

Years have passed since this book, and although it hasn't been easy for my son, he keeps going no matter what. Lately, he's realized everything God has done for him and what he has brought him through. He knows the power of God's written word and understands that God is for him, not against him.

He's in college and will be transferring to a university. He works part-time and drives. These may all seem like simple things anyone can do. But for a boy with an uncertain future from years ago, he is now a young man on the road to fulfilling God's plan and purpose. Hallelujah!

Scriptures

This is my prayer list—subjects I petitioned God for during my son's stay at that special place. These scriptures may not always coincide with my petition, but it's where the Holy Spirit led me. Every one of these petitions has been answered.

No cancer in brain nor spine – Exodus 15:26; Deuteronomy 7:15; Psalm 103:3-6; Matthew 4:24; Mark 1:34

Gain weight – Psalm 104:15

Not lose any weight – Jeremiah 30:17; Jeremiah 33:6

Desire to eat more – Psalm 78:25; Daniel 1:12

To be normal again – Psalm 105:24; Psalm 133:3

Good blood count always – Proverbs 15:30

Good reports from scans/whole body – Proverbs 15:30; Proverbs 25:25; Isaiah 53:1; Isaiah 54:17; III John 1:12

No growth/no tumors – Psalm 91:3; Isaiah 52:7

All abnormal cells gone – Psalm 33:4; Isaiah 53:1 and 4-5

Level changes for good – Psalm 33:18-19; Proverbs 15:30

Good eyesight – excellent – Ecclesiastes 6:9; Ecclesiastes 11:9; Matthew 20:34

Good balance – perfect – Psalm 26:3

Good speech – excellent – Psalm 34:13; Proverbs 16:24

Excellent mind – sharp – Romans 12:2; Philippians 4:7; II Timothy 1:7

No side effects, now nor in the future – Isaiah 54:17; II Corinthians 10:4

No chemo – Proverbs 17:22; Ezekiel 47:12

Healthy bowels – Colossians 3:12

Increase fluid intake – Psalm 29:3; Psalm 42:1

No nausea/vomiting – III John 2

No more headaches – Psalm 23:5; Psalm 24:7; Psalm 110:7; Ephesians 4:22-23

No weakness/fatigue – Romans 8:26

No negativity – Ephesians 4:27; James 4:7

Prayer Chain – Matthew 18:18-20; Colossians 4:2

Wisdom/Guidance – Psalm 91:1; Proverbs 3:5-6; Proverbs 4:7

No setbacks and no surprises – Jeremiah 29:11; Jeremiah 31:17

Peace – Psalm 29:11; Psalm 37:37; Ecclesiastes 11:10

Cooperation and obedience – Jeremiah 31:33-34

Guard heart – Psalm 27:14

Happiness – Proverbs 3:13-18

Looks – Daniel 1:4

Upcoming scans – Proverbs 15:30; Isaiah 52:7

Physicians moving forward – Colossians 4:14

School – Ezekiel 47-22-23; Galatians 3:24-27

Finances – Proverbs 3:9-10

Medications – Proverbs 17:22; Ezekiel 47:9-12

No fear – Psalm 56:3-4

Seed – Jeremiah 30:10

Treatments – Ezekiel 47:12

No organs will be affected – Psalm 34:20; Psalm 51:6; Psalm 139:13

Printed in the USA
CPSIA information can be obtained
at www.ICGtesting.com
LVHW010743080924
790209LV00013B/755

9 798890 415691